A Rationale for

BLACK CHRISTIAN

LITERATURE

— An Essay —

Rev. Walter Arthur McCray

BLACK LIGHT FELLOWSHIP

2859 W. WILCOX ST. • CHICAGO, IL 60612

POST OFFICE BOX 5369 • CHICAGO, IL 60680

312.722.1441

BLACK LIGHT FELLOWSHIP
2859 W. WILCOX ST. • CHICAGO, IL 60612
POST OFFICE BOX 5369 • CHICAGO, IL 60680
312.722.1441

ISBN: 0-933176-14-7

LC: 92-72557

Printed in the United States of America.

Contents

Publisher's Note — "As It Was, So It Is." iv.

Preface vii.

Introduction 1

1 — **Whence Came Black Christian Literature?** 4
2 — **What Is Black Christian Literature?** 8
3 — **Why Perpetuate Black Christian Literature?** 20
4 — **What Purposes are Served through Black Christian Literature?** 26

  1. Nurtures an affection for Scripture and the Lord
  2. Establishes Black identity and unity
  3. Furthers a healthful psychology of Christian Blackness
  4. Bridges the sacred/secular dichotomy
  5. Assists Black Christian integrity
  6. Strengthens the Church's teaching ministry
  7. Facilitates discussion on Black survival
  8. Supports evangelism
  9. Helps the instruction and devotion of Black families
  10. Serves as curriculum materials for Black Christian education
  11. Leads to Black Christian institutions of higher learning
  12. Guides Black Christian organizations
  13. Furthers Christ-centered Black nationhood
  14. Aids Black economic power
  15. Provides an outlet for expressing gifts
  16. Spurs Black folks to read

Conclusion 53

Notes 55

Publisher's Note

As It Was, So It Is.

A Rationale for Black Christian Literature 1985, 1992

There are some older books and notes which, after having gone out of print, need to be recirculated. And they need to be republished with only minor editorial changes. This is the idea behind **"As It Was, So It Is."**

Let us explain. Many older books maintain their value. Though a book's material may be somewhat dated, its overall message may still need to be heard. The message needs to be heard by newer generations who have never heard it. It also needs to be heard by older generations who have yet to fully learn and appreciate its worth.

There is quite an explosion of knowledge taking place as the 21st century approaches. African Americans are writing and reading as never before. It would take a tremendous amount of resources and energies to bring the message of some older books right to the intellectual cutting edge of the times. Major portions of some books would have to be completely rewritten. Black writers and small independent publishers do not always have the human resources, time, or finances to commit to such editorial projects. So the choice is made to tackle fresh and new ideas, and, in historical continuity, to advance the ideas addressed in older writings.

"As It Was, So It Is" alerts the reader that this is a book being recirculated with minor editorial changes. On the other hand it may be a new work in the form of underdeveloped research notes and ideas. This kind of work may prove useful to others who can find the time and energy to further develop these notes and ideas. Alerting our readers to not-so-current publications is preferred to the practice of some publishers who reprint and represent older works as though they expressed the most current knowledge on the subject. The practice fringes on dishonesty and does a disservice to readers and researchers. Many an uncritical book buyer has been misled by a book's new cover and incomplete history of publishing dates and information.

We choose to be forthright in our publishing policy. We want our readers to know beforehand what they are buying.

Keep several thoughts in mind when you read "As It Was, So It Is" publications.

First, over the years the author has become more knowledgeable and matured. In some instances his ideas have substantially advanced beyond what has been written on these pages. In other instances his beliefs and convictions have intensified.

Second, "African American" appears to be the identification term of choice for most Americans of Black racial African ancestry.

Third, African-centered thought and education is becoming pervasive in many educational settings and is being addressed more and more by Black writers of all persuasions, Christian and otherwise. The current interest in the lands and peoples of Africa's Nile Valley, particularly as the point of departure for the origins of humanity and the roots of first civilizations and foundational learning, is most welcomed. Our day is coming back again.

Fourth, there are many cultural and social changes taking place. Information written in the experiences of previous Black generations must be reconsidered within the reformed historical, cultural, and social context of our present day.

Fifth, much of Black reality in America has not changed or has changed for the worse. Racial concerns are yet at the forefront for Black peoples faced with the realities and notions of white supremacy and racism throughout the world. Amidst such a reality, an older Black publication may conceivably remain a very relevant literary treasure due to its incisive analysis and prescriptions addressing issues of race.

Sixth, "Jesus Christ is the same yesterday, today and for ever" (Hebrews 13:8, RSV). His Gospel is "eternal" (Revelation 4:6). His message is timeless, though our understanding of this message is ever growing. Not to exclude others, we who are engaged in Christ-centered Black biblical studies can depend on the Word of Christ.

So, **"As It Was, So It Is."** Enjoy your reading.

BLACK LIGHT FELLOWSHIP
Publisher

Preface

I would like to thank the *National Black Christian Students Conference* for granting **Black Light Fellowship** the permission to republish this work in its present form. It was through the organization's founder, *Ruth Lewis Bentley*, that I was granted the opportunity, in her stead, to share the seeds of this message with a group of Black Christian educators. We will not soon forget how the Lord's Spirit fell upon that small gathering, and brought freedom, awakening, and inspiration to those who received our message. It is my hope that **A Rationale for Black Christian Literature** will educate and move its readers just as that original group of Christian educators was blessed.

I am also grateful to *Olivia S. Chase* for eagerly finding the time to proofread this manuscript.

Reverend Walter Arthur McCray

A Rationale for

BLACK CHRISTIAN

LITERATURE

— An Essay —

Rev. Walter Arthur McCray

BLACK LIGHT FELLOWSHIP
2859 W. WILCOX ST. • CHICAGO, IL 60612
POST OFFICE BOX 5369 • CHICAGO, IL 60680
312.722.1441

Introduction ————

Recently I found reason to rework my resume bringing it to a status concurrent with my present social involvements and ambitions. When I came to the place for stating my vocational objective, this is what I wrote: "To develop a wholistic curriculum of Biblical Christian Black education through which Black American people may be strengthened."

I am proud to say that this objective is my life-goal. It is my conviction that writing Biblical Christian Black literature is my calling from Jesus, my Lord and Liberator. And it is this conviction which I am pursuing and determined to reach with all the energies, resources and grace which the Lord affords.

For this reason I am indebted to the Lord and appreciative before you, my readers, for the opportunity to develop this presentation: "A Rationale For Black Christian Literature." Furthermore, I would hope to present a good and orderly account of those things around which an increasing number of us Black Christians center our lives, and why we do it.

A "rationale" is an explanation of the fundamental reasons for something. It is an exposition of the principles or logical basis of a thing. As applied to the subject before us, this rationale states to us clearly and systematically the essential and good foundation on which Black Christian educational material stands. Such a statement makes known to us what inspired the creation of Black Christian literature; it explains the true nature of Black Christian literature and so gives us a working definition of the subject; it provides for us reasons why such writings should be perpetuated; and it teaches us how Black Christian literature serves its immediate constituency.

Immediately a question may be raised in our minds. Why must Black Christians present what appears to be a "defense" of the kind of literature we compose, trust and teach, when other Christians take their literature and its virtues for granted? In response, merely let me say that such is life, especially for Black-American people. And as one bit of wisdom has it, "if a thing is not worth struggling for, it is not worth much at all."

*I*n the course of considering this rationale, we are confident that Black believers will find good reason commending them to take a strong stand in defense of Black Christian literature. Taking such a stand is hereby encouraged and in fact naturally and specifically becomes our responsibility. If, as Black Christians, we do not become supportive of the written products of our own thinking, who will? But let us not lose heart on account of the apologetical posture we ought to adopt. An apologetic is also a proclamation! When, as Black believers, we defend where we stand, we will also promote what we believe. And the result of this process—stating our own formal justification for Black Christian literature—can do nothing but aid us as Black Christians in our ongoing cause.

As a collective body of writings, Black Christian literature stands to lose without a proper rationale. This is especially so since in these times every written thing worth anything is philosophically put to the test and, therefore, if it wills to survive, must seize its own place of viability within the volatile milieu of multitudinous publications. Black Christian leaders and authors must be reminded that in our day not many ideas and thoughts are accepted without question or qualification. Neither are our Black Christian beliefs! This means we must do our homework if we want our efforts to flourish. A portion of that homework requires laying a proper foundation for our convictions. When Black Christians, especially those of us who are Black Christian writers, find consensus to collectively gather around a "kornah of confirmation" such as this rationale, we shall come to find and appreciate mutual support for our endeavors.

With these preliminary thoughts in mind, let us pursue our subject.

– 1 –

Whence Came

Black Christian Literature?

A brief word about the historical and motivational beginnings of Black Christian literature is in order. From what origins or sources has this literature sprung? To what things can we attribute the formation of Black Christian writings?

It should be noted that in this essay the author is not addressing the formation of Black Christian literature from the earliest beginnings of the Christian faith in New Testament times to the spread of Christianity among Black and African peoples throughout the world. The contributions of Black writers of the Bible Itself, as well as the African ancestry of early Church fathers is successfully being argued in our day. Here we are discussing the presence of Black Christian literature in the American context.

*T*he existence of Black Christian literature is historically rooted in the religious experience of Black people in America. To whatever extent our Black forebearers in slavery, suffering and oppression reduced their experience to writing, expressed with their accompanying consciousness of Christian beliefs and spirituality, is the same extent to which Black Christian literature has existed.

This is not to say that our Black forebearers wrote with a deliberate determination to create a "class" or "body" of Black Christian literature as such. It is only to say that whenever our people sought to make God-sense of their experience, and, with the intent to inform and educate, communicated the same through writing, they were creating Black Christian literature, though formally not regarded as such. A sermon manuscript, a spiritual, a letter, etc. would reflect this point. Other examples might be those occasions where speeches, addresses, articles, etc. were written.

Though not falling into that class of literature which we strictly define as "theology," by attempting to make a definitive statement about the Christian faith and experience, these writings can nevertheless be classified as Black Christian literature. In what way? Inasmuch as the consciousness of Black writers was so pervaded with the things of the Lord, and the things of the Lord were so integrated with the whole of their experience, this theological and spiritual dimension of their lives naturally became imbued in whatever they wrote.

In this context it seems superfluous to talk about a

"rationale," at least a formal one, for the historical development of Black Christian literature. Historically, the spirit which motivated the writing of this literature was basically the natural result of a Black people's orientation around Jesus and His teaching.

*I*n later years, Black Christians sought to make formal expositions of their experience with the Lord. Their writings provided needful information and a sense of understanding and guidance for their fellow believers and their posterity. This effort toward explicating Christian Blackness continues in our generation.

In our day there is an emergence of Black Christian thought being exposited by aggressive and assertive Black believers. By their writings these believers are making conscious and decisive attempts to record the contributions of Black Christians of times past, to make God-sense of the Black experience, and to unveil the significance of the Christian faith from a Black perspective.

Hence, Black Christian literature has come into being through Black Christianity—the Black Church institutionalized and non-institutionalized—and because Black believers sought, and are still seeking, to express through the medium of the written page what they believe and how they feel about God's dealing with them personally, racially and ethnically.

It is the contemporary manifestation of Black Christian literature which the author specifically has in mind as he grapples with this subject. The present-day formation of writings by Black believers needs precise definition and sure grounding if it is to be utilized effectively according to its best and greatest potential.

– 2 –

What Is

Black Christian Literature?

*T*he question attempting to define the precise nature of Black Christian literature is not meant to insult our experience or intelligence. When we ask "What is Black Christian literature?", our asking is meant to challenge us to think deeper about the subject.

*I*nitially, let us place the foregoing question into focus. When reference is made to Black Christian "literature," we are describing specifically Black Christian "educational materials." In this regard, all written Black Christian educational materials can be classified as Black Christian literature, but not vice versa. It can be argued, and this author grants it, that all literature is "educational" in some way or another. Yet, not all writers of literature are didactic in aim or in presentation.

Frequently when the term "literature" is used descriptively of a body of writings, the aesthetic value of the writings is at the core of the definition. Such writings are judged according to the senses of the reader measuring the "beauty" or the "good taste" of the material. However, what we are getting at primarily (though not exclusively) in this discussion are the writings of Black Christian authors who have set out to Christianly educate their readers. Consequently, the materials they create are foremost "instructional" and "informative" materials, and are used in church and academic settings accordingly.

By our use of the designation "literature," we do not intend to limit the purview of this discussion only to written compositions exclusively. The subject being treated also gathers within its scope other forms of educational materials and mediums of communication such as films, filmstrips, records, tapes, etc. In the case of these instructional materials, the subject of Black Christian literature addresses the preparatory "script" underlying and used in the formation of these communicative mediums.

Hence, in treating this subject the terms "literature" and "educational materials" are used interchangeably, and the use of either refers both to compositions intended for reading, and, when applicable, to the written sources underneath and supporting audio/visual tools.

*W*hat then is "Black Christian literature?" In addressing the spontaneous response, and apparently obvious answer, which this question provokes in our minds, we affirm: yes, instructional material that is written by persons who are Black Christians does enter it into competition as Black Christian literature. Of this position let us be firm, sure and forthright from the beginning. Black Christian authorship is the fundamental prerequisite for Black Christian literature. This central tenet is the indispensable premise which qualifies the content of our subject, and upon which any concrete definition of Black Christian literature must be founded and contextualized. Without Black Christian authorship, the treatment of this subject becomes elusive and fizzles from its inception.

The author realizes that this argument has a two-sided ramification. While it focuses Black Christians on the essential role they must play in the development of Black Christian literature, it concurrently tends to raw the sensitivities of white Christians whose writings are geared toward Black people. Should the writings of white Christians for Black people be regarded as "Black Christian literature?" Obviously, this question poses a problem of classification, and for some persons disrupts their understanding of Black identity and the gravity of the Black struggle.

In this regard, our sentiment is that we prefer to label such writings of white Christians either as "white Christian literature for Blacks," or as (ambiguously, but provokingly) "white Black Christian literature," or by some other acceptable yet definitive designation. These terms reflect an essential distinction between the writings of Blacks and the writings of whites, and is necessary for the sake of reality, honesty and clarity. Therefore, we reserve our usage of "Black Christian literature" as the designation immediately and exclusively descriptive of the products of Black Christian authors, and to which we attribute certain basic characteristics.

*R*eturning to the thrust of our position, Black Christian authorship is vital to the development of Black Christian literature. This is its point of origination. Y e t, if some of the words, phrases, images and expressions of white Christian educational materials are merely copied and made cosmetically and superficially "Black" by Black writers, then can we still assert that the literature is therefore "Black"? Of my own convictions, which are shared in common among many serious students of Blackness, poor copies of white Christian educational materials in Black skin do not qualify in actuality as Black Christian literature, regardless of their Black authorship. This is yet another way of saying that not all Black Christian literature which is represented to be such actually is.

The stressing of this point is not a matter of semantics. Approaching the heart of our discussion, this criticism probes the question of the substantive character underlying the writings of Black believers. Many Black Christian educators (the term is being used vocationally, not occupationally) who are familiar with contemporary expositions of Black writers in the field of Christian education (and of white authors who purport to write "Black" material in the same sense as Black authors!) know all too well that historical and in depth Black content is lacking in much of what has been written. Some of these writings are even anti-Black! This assessment could be demonstrated by examining the underlying cultural and social values of such literature. Though for well-founded reasons these Black Christian educators often do not publicly or pointedly voice their criticisms; yet, they are disappointed with what they read and sometimes will privately express their feelings.

Thus we are compelled by our consciences to be truthful and honest with ourselves. Within our souls we are brought to ask, what "genuinely" is Black Christian literature?

On the basis of our studied judgment, we are persuaded by the point of view that genuine Black Christian literature is educational materials which are Christianly written by and for Black people, spurred by Black motivations, filled with Black content, shaped by Black aspirations, set within Black contexts, and achieve Black values and goals. This literature teaches us that Black folks, their personhood, their identity, their culture, their experience, their religion and their future, have value in the sight of God our Creator. Furthermore, Black Christian literature teaches us that Black persons were born, nurtured and cultured Black before they became born again and transformed into a new creation. Consequently, it views our Blackness as a God-given and God-graced human and ethno-cultural essence which is neither eradicated nor suppressed when we get saved, but that which, as some "good thing," is redeemed and brought to wholistic fulfillment through Jesus.

This is our essential definition of Black Christian literature and expresses the substance of those writings of Black believers which are qualitatively Black and are thereby recognized as such. To this position we hold unashamedly and consecratedly.

*T*hus far we have dealt more with the Black side of Black Christian educational materials, but what about their "Christianness?" There are some Black Christians who judge the writings of Blacks by the standards set by the writings of white Christians. To the degree that the written creations of Black believers conform to the writings of white Christian authors is the degree to which these believers consider Black writings more or less "Christian."

Any child of God who is historically knowledgeable of the beliefs and practices of white Christians immediately should detect the flaws in this kind of comparison. So also should the serious student of contemporary white Christian thought. Racist views are yet present within the dogma of white Christianity! I would suggest to you, my readers, that many of the social values present within white Christian literature have traditionally reflected more of the European-American lifestyle and way of doing things than "The Way" of the Lord. Consequently, much of the blindness and inadequate responsiveness of the white Christian community to racism and social inequities in our society can be traced to this point.

It would take a major discussion on this matter in order to portray an adequate picture of the inconsistencies present within white American Christianity and its literature. To do otherwise is to hurt our criticism and our cause. Too often the superficial treatment of this subject causes the intellectually serious Black infidel to mock Black Christians for their naivete. Shallow treatments of this subject have also served only to reinforce white Christians in their blindness. The "light" that is really darkness can be purged from the soul it masquerades only by the forceful conviction of the truth by the Truth (cf. Matthew 6:23).

Though a major discussion of the failures of white Christianity in this country is necessary for some (the inconsistencies are quite obvious for others), this is not the thrust of the present discussion. Nevertheless, any examination of the Christian character and content of Black literature must be based upon a standard more trustworthy than the writings of white Christians. Black Christian literature deserves and is worthy of a value-judgment standard of the highest order. Might not this noble standard be that expression of Christianity practiced by Black Americans as tried and proven in the crucible of American slavery? Not many Black believers would deny the worth and appositeness of this criterion for any examination of Black Christian literature.

At any rate, permit me to give a positive but brief affirmation descriptive of the Jesus whom, as Black believers, many of us preach. We will also present the social implications of His Gospel as we understand them.

*G*enuine Christian literature must be centered in Jesus, who He was, and what He came to do. As the God-man who came to tabernacle among humanity, Jesus grew up as a tender plant, like a root out of dry ground. He was despised and rejected by men. Jesus was a man of sorrows and acquainted with grief.

The Lord whom we serve was born into a poor family, lived some of His most impressionable years in Egypt, Africa, and dwelt in Nazareth—a city whose residents imaged a people possessing little potential. Jesus grew up under oppression. But rather than identifying with the oppressors and their trappings, Jesus chose to identify with the poor, the powerless, the oppressed, and the dispossessed. His close associates were an ignoble and motley band of uneducated persons whom he loved completely, devotedly and faithfully.

The Jesus whom we serve was filled with the Spirit of

the Lord. He was moved with compassion for the misdirected and leaderless masses, and so taught them how to survive their plight. Within Jesus' strategy for ministry and the burden of His message we discover a deep intensity and concentrated focus He had for the poor. Jesus was a preacher—a prophetic preacher. He preached righteousness and justice, in both its personal and social manifestations. He prophesied the destruction that awaited an ungodly generation, and He warned men to prepare themselves to face God's eternal judgement. Further, Jesus also proclaimed release to the captives, the recovering of sight to the blind, healing for the brokenhearted, freedom to the oppressed, and the day of God's salvation—a message pregnant with radical, imminent, and contemporary social implications.

Jesus was a minister; He came to serve. With the abiding presence of God, Jesus went about doing good and healing all who were oppressed by the devil. He taught his followers to care for those who hungered and thirsted, to provide for the homeless and the clothesless, and to visit the sick and prisoners.

The Jesus whom we preach was treated with contempt and suffered wrongfully. In contemporary slang he would be called a "nigger." He knew existentially the meaning of "the cross," with its demand that He die self-sacrificially for God's children by creation. In the prime of His life Jesus was crucified, eliminated from life as a common criminal by those in power who sought to destroy Him and the revolutionary dimensions of His Gospel.

Moreover, our Lord also knew by experience the reality of the resurrection, a resurrection that was not only in the future plan of God, but an eschatalogical resurrection whose power and reality was foreshadowed in the present and rooted in His person. For He said, "I am (presently, right here and now) the resurrection and the life" (John 11:25).

*F*rom this Biblical albeit brief depiction of Jesus, we witness of Him. Therefore, if our literature is to be Christian, it must portray His incarnation as the God-man, His humble beginnings, His empathic pathos, His experience of and sensitivity to oppression, His Spirit-filled life, His steadfast love for and identification with the poor and other societal "nobodies," His message of salvation and liberation, His prophetic posture, His socially revolutionary Gospel, His ministerial social activism, His compassionate laboring for the masses, His undeserved contempt and suffering, His politically incriminative detractions, His vulgar yet redemptive death, and His powerful and vitalistic resurrection.

*W*riting literature which captures the thrust of Jesus and His teaching is the kind of Biblical substance that makes a literature genuinely Christian. Jesus is the author and subject of the Bible. All Biblical teaching must start and end with Jesus, for He is the "author and finisher of our faith" (Hebrews 12:2a). Jesus is the sole

Redeemer of humanity. "There is salvation in no one else" (Acts 4:12a). Giving witness concerning Himself, Jesus said, "I am the way, the truth, and the life" (John 14:6a).

As may be inferred from this emphasis, the Gospels and the Apocalypse—Matthew, Mark, Luke, John and the Revelation—become primary sources for genuine Christian writings. These Biblical writings record first-hand presentations of the life and teachings of Jesus. Our appeal to these preeminent sources, however, does not cause us to disparage other Scriptural sources within the Protestant canonical tradition. "All Scripture is inspired by God and profitable" (2 Timothy 3:16a).

The Scripture in its wholeness is integral to the formation of a complete corpus of Black Christian litera-ture, and should be used accordingly. Yet, in order to be genuinely Christian, Black Christian expositions of other Old Testament and New Testament sources must encap-sulate the message revealed in the personhood, practices and proclamations of Jesus. Jesus is the central theme of the Biblical message. "The testimony of Jesus is the spirit of prophecy" (Revelation 19:10b). Within all that Jesus was, did and said can be found the germinant key, explicit or implicit, which enlightens the understanding of all Scripture and thematically ties it all together like a seam joins a garment, or a melody underlies a song. Black Christian literary compositions lacking the Spirit and words of Jesus the Christ castrate Black Christian literature, emasculate its message, and carry no potential or offer any hope for redemption—temporal, spiritual, or eternal.

*I*n summary of these points, genuine Black Christian literature is the educational writings of Black believers consistent with Biblical Christianity expressed in Jesus and His Gospel, and indigenous to the Black experience. Our people need to read and digest the kind of literature that is written by Black believers, that highlights the Black presence and the "presence of Blackness" in the Scripture, and which explains with clarity and pertinence to them the Biblical message of Jesus' liberation addressed to every people who are under oppression in the world.

This is the kind of content that must fill our literature if it is to be, and to be called, genuinely both Black and Christian.

– 3 –

Why Perpetuate

Black Christian Literature?

*N*ow let us consider some basic reasons why, as Black Christian writers, we desire to perpetuate the kind of literature under discussion. We do this despite the protestations of some believers who "see" neither Black nor white in the Christian faith, and who see themselves championing the cause of Christian "oneness," with ill-regard for racial distinctives, thus finding no good reason for such a presentation as this. They would rather not see the proliferation of Black Christian literature. Written compositions which they deem to be merely "Christian" would suffice for them. And they feel there are plenty of these writings available for consumption by all Christians, irrespective of any color!

We won't take time in this context to dialog with these brothers and sisters about the Biblical meaning of Christian unity in the context of ethnic diversity. Perhaps on another occasion. Ours is to "stay on the wall" and hope that they will come to understand and take refuge within the beauty and security afforded by Black Christian literary creations.

Toward this end we give four basic reasons on whose grounds we promote the advancement of Black Christian literature. This promotion is done for the sake of Black Christian spirituality, Black theology, a Black Biblical apologetic, and the literati within the Black Church.

*J*ust as there exists what is called the "Black Church" in America, there also exists in this land a unique expression of Black Christian experience which may be referred to as "Black spirituality." By referring to Black spirituality we are conceptualizing an experience which identifies the character and conduct of Black Christians who are under the controlling influence of the Spirit of God. The difference between this and the spirituality commonly expressed among white Christians may be perceived generally in worship style, songs and singing, praying, testifying, approach to cultural and social activities, temperament towards endurance, justice, freedom, etc., and a general world-and-life view.

Christian literature is needed to capture and explicate this Black experience under God. It needs to be recorded for the children of the Black Church, as well as for white Christians—many of whom fail to understand and appreciate what the Lord has done among us as a people. In so doing, Black Christian literature becomes promotive of Black spirituality expressed in redeemed and consecrated Black personhood.

*U*ndergirding the expression of Black spirituality is a Black theology which also is a child of the Black Church. Indeed, there are Black Christian beliefs unique to the experience of the Black Church. They are not unique in the sense of providing extra-Biblical data or divergent translations. These Black beliefs are unique in terms of revealing, from the perspective of the oppressed, an ethno-cultural Biblical exegesis of God with emphasis placed on His liberational redemptive activity, disclosing an insightful and radical interpretation of the Scripture especially applicable in the American context, and highlighting a dimension of social awareness and action based upon a wholistic contemplation of the Scripture.

*N*owadays, Black theology is becoming increasingly noteworthy in theologically academic circles. Yet, this does not mean that Black theology is a recent manifestation. To the contrary, Black theology historically exists within the Black Church. It has not been called "Black theology," and it is not systematized. But it is firmly present within Black Christianity, and has by and large been the dynamic of the Black Church.

Black Christian writers must build upon the understanding which our forebearers have handed down to us through Black theology. For it has served us well and can continue to do so. Black theology fashions the foundational understanding upon which the Black Church is established. Black theology sustains the Black Church in perseverance and faithfulness to her Lord, and it guides the Church in social involvement. Black Christian writers who possess the experience, expertise and necessary resources are saddled with the responsibility for expositing Black theology in such a way that the masses of Black Church men and women can appreciably understand how the Lord has revealed Himself among us. If this endemic Black theology is not carefully recorded, it may be lost.

One reason the "words of God" are available to Christians of our day, and, as the Scripture, are preserved in excellent integrity according to the standard of ancient literature, is because they were written. Believers were guided by the Spirit and took time to write the words of God and to pass them along. In the final book of the Scripture Jesus gave this command to His servant John: "write what you see in a book and send it..." (Revelation 1:11, cf.19).

As Black Christian writers, we affirm that the Bible which we now possess, the 66 books of the Old and New Testaments of the Judaeo-Christian Protestant tradition, is God's final Word to humankind. We are under no delusion that what we write is comparable to the Scripture. Nonetheless, this historical ground of our faith does not dissuade us from seeing the importance of our task.

One way to help our brothers and sisters maintain a consecrated respect for the Holy Scripture is to preserve and promote its understanding through our writings. Black Christian writings can provide the kind of contextual understanding surrounding the Scripture that will assist Black Bible readers in approaching it with respect and trust. Our writings can also make it conducive for students of the Scripture to appreciate its continued relevance to their personal needs and its contemporary applicability to social issues. Black Christian literature serves to maintain the freshness of the Word, especially for Black people.

Perhaps the words which Jesus spoke to John ought to become the charge for Black Christian writers: "Write what you see as Black Christians, and send it to the Black Church." Black Christian literature must continue to exist in order that it might become a supportive apologetic for the Word of God being proclaimed in the Black community.

A wise proverb says, "we become what we read." Those things which fill the mind of a man also fill his life. The Scripture teaches us that accordingly as a man thinks in his heart, so is he (Proverbs 23:7).

In the light of this reality, we ask the question: As Black Christian leaders, how do we desire the lives of Black believers to develop? What do we want Black Christians to become? Do we want Black Christians to become "white" in their consciousness and views about life? Won't this be the natural result if their Christian diet consists only of literature written by white Christians from their perspectives? Also, do we want Black Christians to develop reasoning patterns where their functioning in life is concurrently sacred and secular? If the reading materials they use and refer to are solely the products of Black intellectuals who are not Christian-minded, won't this be the outcome?

Black Christian leaders who cherish and strive to achieve high ideals in the lives of their followers will find that Black Christian literature is supportive of their aspirations. Black Christian leaders must write if they are to properly maturate those followers of theirs who are seeking to satisfy their desires for "mind-food" by turning to the printed page. Without the viable option of Black Christian literature, to what reading materials will intellectually inclined Black Christians turn? Black Christian literature must continue to be perpetuated for the sake of the increasingly literate constituency of the Black Church.

– 4 –

What Purposes Are Served Through Black Christian Literature?

*U*nderlying this discussion is an implied relevance which Black Christian literature holds in the struggle for liberation by Black Americans. Genuine Black Christian literature inescapably fulfills such a mission by being just what it is. All truly Black Christian literature is inherently relevant to the needs of Black people and can suffice for our spiritual and social progress.

*W*hen our writings are genuinely Christian, they are in their very essence relevant to the strivings of Black people, for they capture and communicate the redemptive work of God toward humanity. Likewise, when our writings are genuinely Black, they are particularly pertinent to Black Americans, for these writings identify with the Black struggle for freedom in this society. As Black Christian literature, we also see at its very core a widespread relevance it has for many diverse peoples of the world who share in suffering and oppression, for whom the Black experience of continuous suffering, oppression, and intermittent deliverances in America serves as a paradigmatic symbol of cultural and ethnical identification.

Genuine Black Christian literature authenticates itself. It shows itself "worthy of the trust" of Black Americans. Particularly, there are several specific purposes which a definitive body of Black Christian educational materials may serve for its immediate African-American constituency. Let's consider them.

– FIRST –

Black Christian literature nurtures among Black people an affection for the Scripture and the things of the Lord by highlighting the Black presence within the Bible.

Many Black persons, believers and non-believers, do not realize that there is a pronounced Black presence represented among the people of God as recorded in the Bible.[1]

In scanning this Black Biblical data, reference can be made to Cush the grandson of Noah, the father of Nimrod; Hagar, Sarah's Egyptian handmaid; Joseph's sons Ephraim and Manasseh born to his Egyptian wife; the mixed-multitude which left Egypt with the Hebrews under the leadership of Moses; the marriage of Moses to a Cushite woman; the nation of Ethiopia who shall stretch out her hands to God; the Queen of Sheba, coming to visit King Solomon; the Shulammite woman who said "I am Black and beautiful;" Ebedmelech, the Ethiopian who rescued Jeremiah from the pit; the prophet Zephaniah who was the son of Cushi; Jesus Whose ancestry was Black, and Who spent some of His most impressionable years in Egypt; Simon of Cyrene who carried the cross of Jesus; the converted Ethiopian Eunuch; prophets and teachers, Simeon called Niger, and Lucius of Cyrene, members of the Church at Antioch; and so on.

A marked emotional warmth and renewed excitement occurs when Black persons, believers especially, are enlightened by grasping what the Bible says about Black people. And faced with the knowledge of the Black presence in the Scripture, we find that the popular notion of the Bible's being the "white man's book" is blunted (at least from the standpoint of Biblical awareness), and that the interests of honest searchers of truth are enhanced.[2]

– SECOND –
Black Christian literature provides a basis for establishing Black identity and Black unity.

The same kind of information, referred to above, noting the Black presence in the Scripture, also yields the by-product of affirming Black identity and promoting Black unity.

It was the voluminous proliferation of Black literature and studies emerging in the '60s which fueled Black consciousness, self-appreciation and social militancy. Many Blacks, who previously had been ashamed of themselves, consequently found a renewed identity along with an appreciation for the Black group. They also became involved in the struggle for civil rights and freedom. Black Christian literature can achieve the same effect. Perhaps it can do an even better service, because the Scripture, on which this literature is based, addresses more fundamental human issues.

It was through contemplative Biblical reading and serious Biblical study that some Blacks came to a keen sense of personal and group identity. I was one such person. The Bible has radicalized my life like no other book I have ever read. Moreover, the Bible has proven to be firmly stabilizing for my life among a generation of young Blacks, many of whom find themselves retreating from Blackness and forsaking its implications and claims on their lives.

The Black identity which the Scripture teaches is rooted in God who has made all persons in His image and after His likeness. It affirms the heterosexuality of humanity in terms of maleness and femaleness. It is promotive of Blackness without being destructive of whiteness nor any other racial or ethnic group of humanity. The Bible teaches us to love our neighbor as we love ourselves. In so doing it promotes a healthy Black self-love. It teaches us the value of our race to God and reveals our own special place in His plan of universal redemption.

The Scripture is also promotive of Black unity. It teaches Black people how to function as a people, as a nation, even as the Hebrews redeemed from slavery also functioned. Its teachings provide instruction for the unity of the person, the family, the Church, and the nation under God. The Scripture, like no other book, teaches us how to "love our people," and respect our cultural heritage. It teaches Black folks how to work together to achieve common goals even when we have personal differences. The Scripture makes it plain that God does not obliterate our ethnic identity. The redeemed nations of the world shall bring their glory and honor as "nations" into the community of heaven. Eternal redemption expressed culturally and ethnically is at the heart of God's program of salvation (Revelation 5:9; 7:9; 14:6; 15:4; 21:24, 26; 22:2).

Coupled with the motif of unity running through the Scripture, we also have the art of writing which in itself is unitive in nature. There is no other communicative medium which serves the purpose of nurturing a solid and lasting unity like writing. This medium provides for the widespread disseminating of ideas and thought patterns which can be further studied and reasoned through by the reader, thereby bringing the reader to the place where he is able to think the writer's thoughts after him.

Through the format of the printed page, the reader is well-positioned to test for approval the writer's argument, thereby bringing himself to give affirmation to what is written. This transference of reasoning becomes in essence a unity of thought. And a unity of Black thought will ultimately lead to a unity of Black feeling and action. It is this kind of unity of Black thought which cannot summarily or easily be distracted or dissuaded by the manipulative monologues of pseudo-intellectual opportunists who are blessed with the gift of gab!

Even if not persuaded by the writer's argument, the detailed information demanded of and provided by the printed page affords the reader the basis for a close examination of the substance underlying the author's reasoning. Whereas, on the basis of his examination, the reader may not find whole-hearted agreement with the conclusions of the writer, he nevertheless may see clearly enough where the author was headed to be of assistance in helping the author to get there or to get somewhere better!

Why cannot Black Christian writers develop a body of Christian Black literature which both teaches the faith, and promotes Black identity and unity at the same time? This is what our people need, and it can be done.

– THIRD –

Black Christian literature furthers among our people a healthful psychology of Christian Blackness.

There is an unhealthful double-soulness existing in many Black Christian circles. It occurs when Black Christians cannot wholistically integrate their Blackness with their Christianness.

In the epistle of James we read that "a double-minded man is unstable in all his ways" (James 1:8). Besides being unspiritual, the double-souled personality is most unhealthful. It causes instability in living the Christian lifestyle. Until a child of God minimizes his double-soulness, he will find increasing frustration and emotional discord in his Christian experience.

Black Christian literature serves to bridge the gap existing in the mind of the individual Black believer between what it means to be Black and Christian. This bridging enables the Black Christian to live with his Black self while growing in the Lord. It teaches him how to live wholistically and consistently as a Black Christian, in whatever social realms he moves and concerning whatever issues he faces.

– FOURTH –

Black Christian literature helps to bridge the sacred/secular dichotomy controlling the minds of many Black believers.

This dichotomous mind-set is manifested among Christians who refer to the "Church world" in contrast to the "real world." They think that in order to become a "good" Christian it is necessary to commit cultural and social suicide. They consider certain of their activities sacred and others secular.

There are Biblical principles of Christian freedom which regulate Christian conduct in areas where the Scripture is not definitive (1 Corinthians 6:12; 10:23). These principles (which the author has elsewhere written on extensively),[3] when applied by the individual believer, enable him to live a lifestyle totally sacred unto the Lord. In this regard the Scripture is clear. It commands us, "whatever you do, do all to the glory of God" (1 Corinthians 10:31).

This teaching is not meant to suggest that any Christian can participate in anything so long as he "sanctifies" it unto the Lord. It does mean that each Christian should be persuaded by his own conscience when considering the principles of Christian freedom. The point is this: everything in which an individual Christian engages ought to be sacred unto him according to the principles of Christian liberty. If by application of these principles an activity is not approved sacred to him personally, then he ought not to be doing it.

Each Black Christian is free in the Lord to participate in culturo-social activities as the Lord so directs. Black Christian literature is needed to highlight this dimension of the Christian lifestyle for Black Christians. Much of white Christian literature is woefully deficient in this regard. Black Christian writers who are sensitive to the culturo-social milieu in the Black community are best qualified to provide guidance for Black believers in these areas.

– FIFTH –

Black Christian literature gives assistance to Black Christian integrity by helping the Black Christian Church and community remain faithful to the Biblical message.

Older Black Christians used to say that they believed the Bible from "kivah to kivah" (cover to cover). No Christian message can have integrity unless what it teaches is consistent with the mainstream of Scripture, and unless it wholistically accepts all the Word. The whole thing!

This is why many Blacks are turned off by Christianity as has been historically practiced by whites. There have been too many inconsistencies. There has been too much perversion of the Word. There has been too much skirting of issues of obvious morality and social justice. There has been too much hypocrisy. To a good degree many of these problems still persist. But this is not the only reason Blacks are turned off.

Black persons also become disenchanted with the Lord and His Black Church because they see too many

Black preachers and teachers using the Word of God for their own personal gain, and for justifying unChristian lifestyles. When these persons see Black churches which are ingrown and insensitive to the communities in which they are located, they lose interest. It is the responsibility of shepherds to feed, not fleece, the sheep. And the people know it.

Black Christian literature serves a prophetic function to white Christianity and the Black Church. The more we use Black Christian literature to teach grassroots persons the straightforward, unadulterated teachings of the Word, the more the Church will be kept in God's order. In this way the Church will command more respect from the people. An enlightened laity helps the Church fulfill her true mission. And Black Christian literature can enlighten the laity of the Black Church.

− SIXTH −
Black Christian literature contributes to the furtherance of Black Christian maturation by strengthening the teaching ministry of the local church.

Though the needs of all Christians are basically similar, local congregations have special needs. So do the neighborhoods they serve. All good pastors desire to see their members grow and work together. They want their people to be complete, and the community of the church to prosper. Few pastors would deny that they are troubled by uneven growth in the lives of their members. In one area a member is strong, in another area he is weak. The pastor wants him whole.

The present dearth of Black Christian literature makes the pastor's options quite limited. The materials he chooses, though being the best available, may still fail to adequately fit his own needs and the needs of his people. Black pastors and teachers need a wide range of materials from which to select literature that is most appropriate for meeting specific needs among their people.

To the extent that a greater quantity of Black Christian literature is made available for the local congregation, the greater chance our pastors will locate just what their flocks can benefit from most. Black Christian literature can be used to tie together the church's teaching program in such a way that spiritual deficiencies in the lives of its members are addressed properly and timely through the Church's teaching curriculum. This will help local churches grow faster and more knowledgeable, and become of greater service to their communities.

Black Christian literature can also aid the pastor in administratively structuring his church program so that each department is mutually strengthened by the others, and all are made to work together toward common goals. A handbook for a local church explaining the church's program in the light of the Scriptural mandates for ministry among the oppressed would go a long way toward helping new members become oriented in the

Christian faith, in their church, and in their church's ministry. Many Black pastors realize that white Christian administrative models do not work very well in the Black Church. We need our own. And through Black Christian literature we can compose our own.

– SEVENTH –
Black Christian literature facilitates discussion among Black Christians concerning issues germane to our survival.

Black Christian literature helps focus our times of discussion. Why should Black Christians waste valuable time discussing subjects which are peripheral to the Black struggle, when our energies can be channeled otherwise? The seriousness of the Black struggle in this country demands the utmost attention from Black Christians.

It is a foregone conclusion that the mass media, controlled by non-Blacks, has not and will not do justice to the cause of Black Americans. As Black people we must inform and inspire ourselves. Our Black churches can become the mechanism through which this communication can take place. A greater number of Black persons gather in Black churches each Sunday and on special occasions than gather anyplace else. Black Christian literature, distributed through our Black churches, can become a major avenue by which our people are continually brought up to date and educated in the things we need to know and do in order to survive with integrity in this society.

We have witnessed the quickening of discussion groups and the willingness of discussants to share deeper personal experiences when Black Christians speak together about topics centering on themselves in relation to their faith. Whether occurring in Sunday School, Bible Class, institutes, seminars, Vacation Bible School, retreats, etc., Black Christian literature can be a plus in the discussion process.

People talk about the things on their minds. Let's put provocative Black Christian thought on the minds of our people.

– EIGHTH –
Black Christian literature strengthens the evangelistic endeavors of the Black Church.

Black non-Believers are more naturally inclined to read evangelistic materials indigenous to the Black experience than they are to read other literature. Christian tracts and pamphlets that are authentically Black can prove very useful in preparing the unsaved for conversion.

On the day of Pentecost, the Spirit of God caused each nation represented in Jerusalem to hear the Gospel proclaimed in its own native dialect. We are hard pressed to explain the reason for such a happening other than this: that the Lord wanted every people to clearly and forcefully understand the message of Jesus, and to consider this message a personal-ethnical invitation of salvation from Him to them. It worked. Thousands of people were saved.

The Pentecost experience provides direction for the development of Black Christian evangelistic literature. In principle, we should desire to do no less than what God caused to be done. Black Christian literature is needed to communicate the Gospel in the language, even in the popularized slang, of Black folks. If it does, then we can anticipate that the Black Church will reap the fruit of conversions even as the first-century Church indigenized the Gospel message.

– NINTH –

Black Christian literature strengthens the devotional and instructional experiences taking place in Black Christian families.

"The family that prays together stays together." There is much truth in this familiar adage. Yet, let us not be shortsighted or ignorant. The Scripture teaches us to pray, not only "with the spirit" but also "with the mind" (1 Corinthians 14:15a). Effective family praying is predicated upon a common understanding among family members. It is the family that learns together which also yearns together!

The kind of devastation which is taking place in the

Black family makes many Black believers keenly aware that much more penetrative analyses and solutions are needed than many of the traditional expositions on the Christian family. For instance, what devotional materials are addressing the needs of the unemployed and underemployed Black males who have a wife and children to support, and whose self-confidence and personal dignity is shattered? What Christian instructional materials speak to the needs of the single Black mother on public assistance, trying to survive at the mercy of meager resources, intimidating gangs, and effeminate Black men? What Black Christian writings have you read lately that have challenged Black parents to rise up in righteous indignation and take charge of their children's "education" (wasting) taking place in the public school system? What writings of Black believers are prophesying about the rampant sexual immorality existing in the Black society, whose roots can be traced to lax standards and unspiritual teaching in the home?

The Black Christian home is in dire need of devotional and instructional materials geared to its special problems. We are losing too many generations of children. Too quickly the fabric holding together Black families is becoming ragged and tearing apart. Providing Black Christian literature for our homes is a positive step in the direction of bringing healing to our families.

– TENTH –
Black Christian literature serves as the cur-

riculum materials for the discipline of Black Christian education and for the development of Black Christian educators.

Many Black believers are following the field of Black Christian education with a new seriousness: Sunday School teachers, directors of Christian education, and pastors on the Church level; professors and students on the elementary, high school and higher education levels; and deans, conference conveners, workshop instructors, congress delegates, and conference participants on the denominational and para-Church levels. All are paying closer attention to the Lord's command, "teaching them to observe all things whatsoever I have commanded you" (Matthew 28:20a).   With an awakened interest, Black Christians are giving the discipline of Black Christian education a closer consideration.

In each of the aforementioned instructional settings there is a need for teaching matter, a basic "text book," which serves as a pool of knowledge to be mastered and a guide to be used in nurturing Christian sentiments in Black Christian learners and educators in training.   In many of these settings there are reexaminations and revisions of course content and objectives taking place. There is a quest by planners for newer, more up-to-date, and more solid information and resources that will do a better job of equipping Black Christian educators for the ministerial work of teaching the Black Christian community.

Obviously, in the midst of such a quest, Black Christian literature manifests a self-evident value for the Black Christian educator (or, as might be said, for the "Christian Black educator", a concept which, to the author, more fundamentally expresses genuine Black Christian being, and toward the center of experience the message and maturation of Black Christian persons is headed). Without Black Christian literature, the teaching of the serious Black Christian educator (that is, the substance of his content) becomes supplemental and adjunct to existing (white) Christian educational materials, and his focus, of necessity, is circumscribed by his personal presentations. His scope remains lecture-centered. On the other hand, with the assistance of Black Christian literature, the teaching of the serious Black Christian educator remains mainstream. That is, by virtue of his course textbook, his content becomes a primary source for his students, and his lectures can send his learners spanning into varied directions for research into a school of contemporary "Black Christian thought" reaching new horizons.

Hence, the development of Black Christian literature strengthens the field of Black Christian education on all levels. Thereby, Black Christian literature contributes to the education of a better qualified and prepared Black Christian educator. The formal education of these Black Christian educators will have been made first-rate for two reasons. One, because its process will be marked by instructors who have at their disposal a qualitative and well-balanced body of instructional materials which serve as the backbone of the curriculum. And two, the courses and presentations of these instructors will be better prepared. By having a better access to needed information, more of their preparation time can be streamlined. Their hearts can rest confidently in the good provision of reliable Black Christian writings.

– ELEVENTH –
Black Christian literature is the forerunner to creating Black Christian institutions of higher learning.

I reside in Chicago. Of all the large Black Churches, of all the leading Black preachers, of all the many Black Christian thinkers in Chicago, there is not one major and accredited Black Christian institution of higher learning in Chicago existing on its own! We leave the instruction of our people in the hands of others. What a waste.

Why? The reasons may be varied. Yet, our Black Churches have the money; we have capable administrators and instructors; we possess the necessary constituency; and we have the facilities. So why? Perhaps we need to be admonished and embarrassed in print.

A school of Black Christian thought will ultimately lead (in Chicago as well as other localities across the nation) to a fully certified, accredited and respectable Black Christian institution – college, seminary, and/or university. For Black Christian literature will move Black Christians in such a way that they will rise up to build a better Black community, and will insure the preservation of what has helped them by institutionalizing what they have learned for the many Black Christian generations that will follow along the path they have trod.

– TWELFTH –

Black Christian literature works both to guard and to guide the development of Black Christian organizations.

There is a growth of Black Christian para-Church organizations geared toward serving the Black community. These organizations need protection and direction. Black Christian literature can provide this service for these organizations.

If the social service of a Black Christian organization is guided solely by the needs of its Black constituency, then its spirit can tend to become merely humanistic without reference to godliness. There also exists the possibility that a Black Christian activist organization, functioning within the milieu of ecumenicalism, can become engaged in harmful syncretistic postures compromising its standard of Christian beliefs.

In this context, Black Christian writings can serve a pastoral function for Black Christian organizations by helping them maintain a sacred focus in serving people, and by guiding their coalitional endeavors with other social service organizations, Christian, religious or otherwise, so that their doctrinal stance remains intact.

The modern rise of Black Christian organizations marks the breaking of novel ground for the Black Church. We see Black Christian organizations making ventures into the areas of politics, economics, counseling, healthcare, employment services, morality issues, international affairs and the like. Many of these organizations are making honest and whole-hearted attempts at alleviating pressing problems existing among the Black populace. This is trailblazing. And this trailblazing needs direction.

The keen and creative insights of Black Christian writers can be invaluable to these pioneering Black Christian organizations. The development of Black Christian institutions is germane toward the survival of our people. But organizations do not develop into institutions overnight, or with little regard to the foundations on which they stand. A body of Black Christian literature specifically addressing itself to the development of Black Christian institutions can fashion the ideology that will guide these institutions into a progressive and blessed future.

The institutional development of Black Christian organizations must be approached carefully. This approach is demanded due to the role played in the community by the premier Black institution, the Black Church. The rise of Black para-Church organizations must not be allowed to harm the perpetuation of the Black Church. The Church is the Lord's primary organism for working in the world. Black Christian writings which clearly define the non-competitive distinctions, in considerations of either nature or service, existing between the Black Church and Black Christian organizations will mitigate any foreseeable causes of strain and of rupture in relations between these complementary institutions.

– THIRTEENTH –
Black Christian literature helps the cause of Christ-centered Black nationhood by delineating a comprehensive curriculum for Black people in America.

One reason Black people, along with many Black "leaders," are so disoriented is because we lack a wholistic objective for the liberation and well-being of our people in this land. And lacking this objective we also lack the curriculum that would help us reach such an objective.

Jesus told His apostles to "make disciples of all nations" (Matthew 28:19). This was a direct command for the disciples to engage in the kind of evangelism and nurture of the Church which took into account the ethno-cultural identity of the evangelized.

The Gospel message is a personal message, but it is in no way an individualistic message. The Gospel is corporate. This means that the Gospel message has not fully run its course until each ethnic family comes to experience what it means to be a people whose lives and ways of living are patterned after the life of Jesus and His "way" as expressed socially.

Among Black believers there is a growing realization of the importance of the Black family to the wholesome growth of Black individuals. Likewise there ought to be a comparable appreciation for the place which the Black nation serves in the nurture of the Black family. Black families need a context for growth and service. This context ought to be Black nationhood centered around Christ Jesus.

If Black Christianity is to further help the cause of Black liberation, then it must do so by describing the nature of Black nationhood guided by Black Christian values. Black people need a wholistic liberation agenda, and Black believers are in a place to provide this agenda. The movement for Black liberation and well-being in this country must be founded upon a well-reasoned and theologically sound ideology. This is the only way it will succeed. We believe that the writing of Black Christian literature works integrally toward accomplishing this purpose.

– FOURTEENTH –
Black Christian literature aids Blacks in the struggle for economic power.

There are significant financial gains to be made through writing, publishing, producing and marketing Black Christian literature. In substantiation of this point, just observe the aggressive ventures of white Christian publishing companies which increasingly are making inroads into the Black Christian market.

All of our churches and Christian organizations use literature. We use it weekly and on special occasions. Each year, millions of Black Church dollars are spent on Christian educational materials. Each time we pay for white Christian publications we are sending money outside of our communities and outside of our control.

The tithes and offerings of Black Church members are too precious and too hard-to-come-by not to be used wisely. With the treasure that has been entrusted to it, the Black Church is capable of doing much more for the benefit of the Black community and our struggle for freedom than it is presently doing. If we used our money to buy Black Christian literature, especially that which is published and produced by Black companies and individuals, we would substantially add to the economic growth of the Black community. Moreover, the propagation of Black Christian literature is needed to further the traditional economic independence of the Black Church.

– FIFTEENTH –
Black Christian literature provides the Black Christian writer with an outlet for expressing his gifts.

The Dead Sea, though very rich, is called "dead" because it is the lowest spot on the earth. Everything flows in, but nothing flows out! The gifts and talents of many a Black Christian are bottled up like the Dead Sea because he has not taken his pen to hand in service for the Lord. Jesus said, "Let your light so shine before men, that they may see your good works and give glory to your Father who is in heaven" (Matthew 5:16). To Black believers we say: Write! Write! Write your Black light!

The excuses and reasons which Black Christians give for not writing abound. "Not enough time." "Too busy." "Not a good enough writer." "Speaking is easier." "Leave that for college trained and seminary students." Etcetera, etcetera, etcetera, etcetera, ad nauseam! In the meantime, the Black Church is denied years of pastoral experience from Black pastors, deprived of keen insights into new horizons from preachers in training, stifled in development because of sloppy teaching and preaching, etc.

Black Christians could exercise more of their potential and reach a higher experience in the Lord if they would only write. Writing on the things of the Lord serves the Black Christian. It sharpens his mind, makes his thinking more sound, releases his pent-up emotions, and inspires his spirit to reach for higher heights. If, as Black Christian writers, we use the talents we already possess, the Lord will then give us more to use. As we serve the Lord, we will serve and increase ourselves.

Writing Black Christian literature can prove to be nothing but a blessing for those Black believers who are willing to obey the Lord and step out on faith in this important and precious ministry.

— SIXTEENTH —
Black Christian literature spurs Black folks to read.

The most common note of despair covering the entire spectrum related to Black Christian literature is this: "Black folks don't read." This cry, and I mean cry, is heard from Black bookstore owners to would-be Black authors.

More often than not, this popular lament that "Black folks don't read" is stated more as a justification for inaction and feeding Black folks media trash than as a simple fact or analysis of a problem. It turns into a self-fulfilling and self-defeating prophecy. Since "Black folks don't read and won't read," then the Blacks who parrot this cop-out don't read, and won't read. Furthermore, these Blacks don't bother to encourage other Blacks to read, and neither will they write.

The mentality that stereotypes the Black populace into illiteracy is cursed. And the Blacks who stubbornly hold these negative opinions and yet are not contributing to correcting this "problem" are accomplices in the continuing subjugation and oppression of Black Americans by white people. How easily it is that we forget the words of Jesus: "you will know the truth, and the truth will make you free" (John 8:31b).

In this context, I will not argue in the debate as to whether or not Black folks read. Let those argue who asininely want to prove that we don't.

My argument is this. First, if Black folks don't read, then we should teach them to read, encourage them to read, and then make them read. Second, if we really want Black folks to read, then we ought to write something Black for them to read. Third, those whose thoughts are contrariwise to these exhortations ought to please get out of the way. We don't need the pacifying mental "dung" of these Black ethnic gainsayers in this eternal life-and-death struggle.

There is a fierce battle for the Black mind occurring everyday in our society. A major battleground for this struggle occurs in the mass media and the marketplace. The mass media and marketplace perpetuation of the products of popular culture and consumerism gets over far too much among Black people. And it gets over not necessarily because of the "worthiness" of these products to be consumed, but because the marketplace and the mass media are flooded with both the products and also the promotions. A demand is created and then it is filled. And the minds of Black folks are a ground all to fertile and available for manipulation and exploitation by the profiteers of the day.

If, as Black Christians, we really believe in the worthiness of our cause, then let us expose to the reading public the writings we have to offer. This is not an appeal to advance our cause by manipulating the masses, but a call to just "show up." Black Christian writers are losing by default because we fail to show up. In response to the exposure of Black Christian literature by Black believers, Black people will read what is made available to them as a viable option to whatever is gaining control of their minds.

Conclusion ──────

*T*he Scripture says that all Christians know "in part" (1 Corinthians 13:12). Too often, the impression that white Christian literature has left on the minds of its readers is that white believers know it all! The emergence of Black Christian literature serves to remind white American Christianity that it does not have a death hold on the truth of God.

God has bestowed a blessing upon His Black Church. He has given Black believers an expression of Himself that is complementary to the truthful insights of white Christianity, and that are invaluable and essential toward a full perception of the Godhead. In contrast to white American theological doctrines imported from Europe, the theological expressions of the Black Church are indigenous to this country. This body of truth must come to its own rightful acceptance in America. Without the offering of Black Christian literature, "American" theology remains impotent to significantly bring about righteous and radical systemic change within this society.

To the extent that Black Christian literature is propagated among Christian circles is the degree to which something of God is propagated among the people of this land. Christian Black literature takes the knowledge of God gained through the Black Christian experience and spreads this knowledge wherever it is read.

*B*lack Christian literature has a message to carry to the world. It is a message of a Black-American people that says God is still in the liberation business. It says that the Church can persevere through the fire of suffering and oppression, because a Black Church was born in the fire of slavery and endured. It says that the Church can sing the songs of the Lord in a foreign land, because a Black Church sings the spirituals. It says that the Church can make something out of nothing, because a Black Church took the no-things in the eyes of the world and, with the help of the Lord, created them into a people precious and special.

The message of Black Christian literature says that the Church can be what it is because a Black Church determines to be, just be, what it is—a Black people with the grace and glory of God written into their hearts and lives.

Notes

----

1. See **The Black Presence in the Bible** *(Vol. 1)* and **The Black Presence in the Bible and the Table of Nations** *(Vol. 2)*. (Black Light Fellowship: Chicago, 1990).

2. Information about early Church fathers who were African, early Church Councils held on Black soil, and the development of the Coptic Church in Egypt also serve a similar purpose.

3. See **Black Folks and Christian Liberty: Be Christian. Be Black. Be Culturally and Socially Free.** (Black Light Fellowship: Chicago, 1979, 1987).

Books by Rev. Walter Arthur McCray

Black Young Adults
How to Reach Them, What to Teach Them (1992)
    (Originally, **Reaching and Teaching Black Young Adults**, 1986)

A Rationale for Christian Black Literature (1985, 1992)

The Black Presence in the Bible *(Vol. 1 - Teacher's Guide)*
Discovering the Black and African Identity
    of Biblical Persons and Nations (1990)

The Black Presence in the Bible and the Table of Nations
    (Genesis 10:1-32) *(Vol. 2 - Table of Nations)*
With emphasis on the Hamitic Genealogical Line
    from a Black perspective (1990)

Black Folks and Christian Liberty
Be Christian. Be Black. Be Culturally and Socially Free!
    (1979, 1987)

Toward a Wholistic Liberation of Black People
Its Meaning as Expressed in the Objectives of
    the National Black Christian Students Conference (1979)

Saving the Black Marriage
Nine vital lessons on Settling, Saving,
    and Solidifying the Black Marriage (1981)

How to Stick Together during Times of Tension
Directives in Christian Black Unity (1983)

BLACK LIGHT FELLOWSHIP
POST OFFICE BOX 5369 • CHICAGO, IL 60680
312.722.1441